A SAINT FRANCIS PRAYER BOOK

Malcolm L. Playfoot

SOMETIME
ADMINISTRATOR OF THE
SOCIETY OF THE COMPANIONS OF
SAINT FRANCIS

GW00674693

First Published in Great Britain in 1941 by
Society for Promoting Christian Knowledge
Holy Trinity Church
Marylebone Road
London NW1 4DU

Thirty-second impression 2002

British Library Cataloguing-in-Publication Data

A catalogue record for this book is available from the British Library

ISBN 0-281-01040-4

Printed in Italy

IT is difficult to say in a few words just what prayer is. If a hundred people were asked, there would be a hundred different answers, yet all with something of the truth in them, according to the spiritual depth and experience of the persons concerned.

To put it very simply, let us say that praying is thinking God's thoughts. That makes us realize that many of our so-called prayers have been unworthy, through selfishness or through a lack of understanding what the Divine thinking is like.

How are we to learn that art of prayer? In just the same way in which any other and lesser art has to be learned—by practice based upon a true model. We have the Divine model in our Lord's prayers, and it is to help with the practising that this little book has been made.

It is far and away the best to learn to pray from the heart without having the need of a set form of words, but our frailty is such that some sort of framework for our thoughts is often a help. There need be no harm in this so long as we remember that the form of words is but a skeleton and nothing more. The prayer is what we clothe upon the bare bones.

So when we say "Let us pray," let us remember the command in the greatest of all the Church's offerings of prayer: Sursum Corda—Lift up your hearts.

STROUD.

O Sapientia, 1940.

CONTENTS

(These prayers are written in a personal form; they may easily be made suitable for common use by slight alterations, the accustomed endings being added as required.)

1. WAKING.

God, who hast kept me through the night, keep me through this day. I am thine, make me thine for ever; thine in heart and mind to do thy will; through Jesus Christ our Lord.

2. WASHING and DRESSING.

O Lord, make me clean within, for there is nothing hid from thee; wash away my sins and let me be pure in thy sight. Cover the nakedness of my weakness with the strength of thy presence, that I may be thine all the day long.

3. MORNING: SUNDAY.

Most gracious Lord Jesus, I wake with joy to praise thee on the day of thy resurrection. Grant that I may rise from my past sins to serve thee anew in holiness of living, and vouchsafe to bless this new week with thy presence.

4. MORNING: WEEKDAYS.

O Lord, let my first thoughts be of thee; to praise and to thank thee for thy goodness and thy protection through the night. Give me thy grace, I pray thee, so to live through this day that at nightfall I may not be ashamed to meet thee.

5. BEFORE WORK.

My God, I can do nothing good without thee; give me, I pray thee, the sure knowledge of thy nearness in all my work today, that doing all things with thee I may serve thee truly; through Christ our Lord.

6. BEFORE GOING OUT.

Hold thou my steps, O God, and govern all my goings; that I may walk in thy ways and accomplish thy will.

7. MIDDAY.

At this half-tide between night and night, do thou, O Lord of Light, bridge the darkness of my sin with the brightness of thy glory; giving thy grace that I may greet the evening in thy continued presence.

8. BEFORE AFTERNOON WORK.

O God, help me to make a new start with the remainder of this day's work; forgiving what has been amiss during the past hours and blessing my fresh efforts.

9. Going Home.

O Lord, my day's work is over; bless all that I have done aright, and forgive all that has been wrong; and for the remaining hours of this day grant me the peace and rest that come from thee alone.

10. Evening.

As this day draws towards its end, do thou, O God, give us all the comfort of knowing that thou art near us; keeping, healing and blessing thy people. What we have done today we offer to thee, giving thee the simple service of our loving hearts.

11. Going to Bed.

Blessed be thou, O God, who makest me to lie down in safety. Keep us all, I pray thee, through the darkness, and wake us with the joyful knowledge of thy continuing love and care; through Jesus Christ our Lord.

12. At Night: Sunday

Add to the blessings of this day, O Lord, thy merciful protection through the night, and give me grace to be more than ever thine in this new week.

13. At Night: Weekdays.

O God, I pray thee to keep us all in thy loving care all through this night, bringing us to the morning refreshed with happy sleep, to be busy again as thou wilt guide and call us.

14. WHEN WAKEFUL.

Whether I wake or sleep, Lord, I am thine. Secure in thy loving keeping teach me to rest in thee, whether I sleep or wake.

15. FOR THOSE WHO WORK WHILE WE SLEEP.

Through the hours of this night, O Lord, I pray thee to bless those who are working. Keep them safe in thy love, accepting the offering of their labours for thy glory and the good of mankind.

16. BEFORE NIGHT WORK.

Jesus, my Lord, do thou keep watch with me through the dark hours, that in the light of thy dear presence I may see clearly what thou wouldest have me to do. Let thy blessing be upon all who serve while the world sleeps, and bring us safely through the darkness to the coming day.

17. GRACE BEFORE MEALS.

Blessed Lord, we pray thee to be present at our table, hallowing thy gifts to our use; that eating to satisfy our needs we may remember those who lack.

18. Grace After Meals.

Give us grace, O Lord, to be ever thankful for thy providence, and hearts always ready to provide for the needs of others.

19. Before Church.

Give me a quiet mind, O God, that I may worship thee with an undivided heart, and grant that in sincerity I may offer thee an acceptable service.

20. After Church.

Lord, I pray thee to accept my worship, forgiving my faults and completing all with thy blessing.

21. For All Preparing for their Communion.

O Lord, hear my prayer for all who make ready to come to the Altar, for the Priest and his helpers, and for all who intend to receive thy most Blessed Sacrament. Give them the help of thy Spirit that they may draw near in a warm faith, and with humble hearts may greet thee, O Lord our Saviour.

22. Preparation for Communion.

In thy great and wonderful mercy to me, a sinner, make me a clean heart, O God, and renew in me the gift of the

Holy Spirit, received in my Confirmation. Grant that I may have left nothing undone, no wrong unacknowledged, no effort spared to be honest in my heart-searching, no sincere attempt at reparation; and in thy love allow me to share in the Blessed Sacrifice.

23. THANKSGIVING FOR COMMUNION.

What thanks can I give thee my Lord, except the offering of my whole life? What way is there for me to show my gratitude but by opening the door of my heart and begging thee to enter and to reign therein? Lord Jesus, come.

24. FOR THE CHURCH.

O Lord Jesus Christ, cleanse and purify thy Holy Church, against which thou hast promised that the powers of evil shall never prevail; revive the ancient fires of devotion and courage, and heal all division with thine own gift of peace.

25. FOR THE PARISH AND ITS PRIEST.

Bless this parish, O God, and grant that we may all work together in united devotion to thee. Give thy Priest grace to lead a holy life, that helped by our sincere prayers he may bring the comforts of thy Church to all thy people, that we may all serve thee in unfeigned love.

26. FOR CHURCH WORKERS.

Bless, Lord, all who work for thy Church, especially in this parish. Grant that they may so agree in love that envy and jealousy may never mar their labours, but that sincere and humble service may merit thy blessing.

27. FOR THE SPREAD OF CHRIST'S KINGDOM.

Almighty God, I pray thee to uphold and to bless all who are giving their lives to spread the knowledge of Christ throughout the world. Give me grace to live so that I may never hinder their work, but may be allowed to help bring near the time when he shall be the acknowledged King of every heart.

28. FOR ALL MEMBERS OF RELIGIOUS ORDERS.

O Lord, give the blessing of thy grace to all members of Religious Orders, that they, with all others who have dedicated their lives to thy service, may offer themselves in disciplined humility to thee, keeping their rules in holiness and pureness of living; through Jesus Christ our Lord.

29. FOR A DISCIPLINED HEART.

Give me a heart that is disciplined in thy service, O Lord; that by wholesome self-control I may be better fitted to obey thy loving will.

30. For Grace to Lead a Life of Prayer.

Lord Jesus, give me grace to live so near to thee that I may constantly find thee in prayer, in every detail of my life trusting thee and seeking thee.

31. For Grace to make a Good Self-Examination.

O God, grant that I may be honest and thorough in my heart-searching, not seeking to hide or to excuse what thou, through the Spirit, wilt reveal.

32. For Strength to Make a Good Resolution.

Blessed be thy name, O God of my salvation, for thou hast led thy servant in the way of truth. Give me a heart to seek thee, Lord, and strength and grace to resolve to follow where thou in thy mercy hast shown the way.

33. For Determination to Keep it.

O Lord, be thou my helper, for without thee I am weak and can never keep what thou hast put into my heart to resolve. Hear me, O Lord, for thy Name's sake, for thou art gracious.

34. For Spiritual Understanding.

O my God, give me the wisdom of a child, that in simplicity I may approach thy mysteries. Give me the understanding of a humble mind, illumined by thy Spirit, and so shall I learn thy ways.

35. For the Revelation of the Will of God.

O Lord, open my heart that I may hear thy voice; show me thy will, O God, and give me grace to follow it for ever.

36. For Gentleness in my Dealings.

Grant me, Lord, to be so much thine that I may fitly show thy presence in all my dealings. Give me thy patience, thy sympathy and thy love, that wherever I may be men may see, not me, but thee.

37. For a New Heart.

Make me a new heart, O Christ; a heart cleansed and purified by loving thee, a heart that shall be ready and prepared for thy coming to rule my whole life, my King and my God.

38. For Grace to Persevere in Prayer.

O Lord, uphold me, I pray thee, and grant that however difficult life may be, however seemingly dark, I may never weary or falter in coming to thee in prayer.

39. For Humility.

Give me a humble heart, O God, that I may see myself as I truly am, stripped of all my pride by thy revealing love, against which no self-excuses can avail. And yet in thy great mercy receive me and cast me not away; for Christ's sake.

40. In Temptation.

Save me, O Lord; hear my prayer, most loving Saviour. My feet slip and I fear to fall; do thou hold me fast in thy keeping and I shall overcome the ememy. In the Name of Jesus Christ I bid the powers of evil begone from me. Blessed be thy Holy Name, Lord Jesus, thou lover of souls.

41. When Conscious of Sin.

God be merciful to me, for I know that I have failed thee. I knew better and still I did wrong. Forgive me, O my Father, and give me thy grace and strength to start again in new hope and trust; through Jesus Christ our Lord.

42. For Work about the Home.

O Lord, I pray thee to bless all that I do in the house or garden. Accept it as an act of worship, and give me grace to find thee in every task and duty, however small or dull they may sometimes seem.

43. For Rest and Recreation.

Bless, O God, the times when work is laid aside, and grant that my hours of rest and leisure may be given to thee, that I may serve thee the better for their pleasure.

44. Before Entertaining Guests.

O Lord, I pray thee ever to be my first guest, that my friends may find thee in my home. Give us thy gift of happy friendship, and do thou control our thoughts and words by thy blessed presence.

45. Before Going Shopping.

Help me, O God, to spend wisely and to buy fairly, remembering that money and the things of this world are a trust for which I shall have to give an account to thee.

46. Before Undertaking New Work.

Go with me, Lord Jesus, and help me to start this work in thy spirit, for without thee I must surely fail.

47. Before Reading a Serious Book.

Grant, O Lord God, that I may read with eyes and mind enlightend by thy Spirit, that I may use thy gifts in the service of my fellows, to thy glory, O thou in whom is all truth and all beauty.

48. Before a Journey.

Take my footsteps into thy keeping, O God, and lead me into the paths of everlasting life. Grant me a safe journey and a blessed return; through Jesus Christ our Lord.

49. Before Reading the Bible.

Make my heart ready, O God, to receive thy words, that, reading by the light of the Spirit, I may be enabled to discern what thou willest me to learn.

50. After Reading the Bible.

Grant, O God, that I may not have read thy Word in vain, but that my life may show what thou in thy mercy hast taught me.

51. For the Ministry of Angels.

O Lord, as thy holy Angels ministered to thee upon earth, grant us their help in all our needs, that their loving care may keep us safe and draw us to thee whom they worship unceasingly, looking upon the unclouded brightness of thy face.

52. When Feeling Unwell.

O Lord, I pray thee give me the help of thy presence, that by thy healing power I may be perfectly restored to health and wholeness, to serve thee without hindrance of mind or body.

53. WHEN TIRED.

Beloved Lord, I am weary. Teach me how to rest in thee; that, trusting thee in all things, I may share thy strength and partake of thy promised refreshment.

54. FOR COURAGE.

Take my hands, O my Master, and give me strength to overcome my fears; deepen my trust, and they shall vanish away. I will lift up mine eyes to thee, and in thy power I shall go onward in thy way. Blessed be God who giveth us the victory.

55. FOR SIMPLICITY.

Take from me, O God, the complexity of desires and thoughts that belong to this world. Give me again the heart of a child, that in simple love I may hear thy voice; and the trust of a child, that, hearing, I may come to thee.

56. FOR A GREATER SENSE OF BEAUTY.

Open my eyes and my ears, O Lord my God, that I may see and hear more clearly the loveliness that thou hast put into the world, and give me grace, I pray thee, to show in my turn some of thy gifts in my life, to thy glory.

57. ON HEARING BAD NEWS.

Hold thou me up, O God, and give me all the strength that I shall need. Let

thy holy angels be my helpers to keep
and to sustain me; and I pray thee to
strengthen my trust in the nearness of thy
love; through Christ our Lord.

58. FOR SINCERITY.

God, make me single and sincere; take
away all that is not true, all that hinders
thy work in me; for only so shall I serve
thee.

59. WHEN WAITING.

Teach me, O Lord, to be patient, and
help me to use every minute in thy service,
that of thy gifts nothing may be lost or
wasted.

60. FOR MAKING A BETTER USE OF TIME.

O my God, all my life is thine; help me
so to plan and arrange the hours of this
day that I may serve thee in them all,
for they are thine.

61. BEFORE AN IMPORTANT DECISION.

O Lord, show me how to decide, and
give me such trust in thee that I may
receive thy guidance, and in calmness may
act upon it.

62. FOR CHARITABLE THOUGHTS.

Let thy love be my love, O Christ; may
I see with the eyes that thou hast opened.

Take away all jealousy and unkindness, all hardness and intolerance, that in simple and quiet service I may best please thee.

63. BEFORE FACING AN UNPLEASANT SITUATION.

O Lord, I beg thee to take away my dread of what I have to do; give me, I pray thee, grace to think and act in perfect charity, without regard to my own painful feelings, but only considering what is thy will.

64. FOR INCREASED FAITH IN THE POWER OF PRAYER.

Lord, I believe that thou indeed hearest my prayer, and hearing, answerest. Help thou mine unbelief and my unwillingness to come to thee in prayer. Though my faith is so weak, yet do thou receive my petitions that I make in thine own name, Jesus Christ our Lord.

65. WHEN IN SPIRITUAL DARKNESS.

Lord, I am very dear to thee; this I know only since thou sayest so. Be thou very near to me, and make me know it by telling me so.

66. AN ACT OF ADORATION.

My God, I adore thee. In thy goodness, in thy love, in thy mercy, I worship thee. I bow before thee, in wonder doing homage

to thy loving majesty. O my God, I adore
thee.

67. AN ACT OF DEDICATION.

I am thine, O God; take me and make
me thine for ever. Thou art mine; O
God, forsake me never, for I am thine.

68. FOR FRIDAY.

Almighty God, so rule my heart that
I may never fail to be gratefully mindful
of the Passion of thy dear Son. Teach
me to live that I may show in my own
life the life of him who died for us all,
Jesus Christ our Redeemer.

69. FOR THE GRACE OF THE HOLY GHOST.

O blessed Spirit, the source of all life
and all holiness, enlighten my eyes that
I may know thee, give me grace that I
may love thee; that knowing and loving
thee I may both seek and find thee, and
in thy light may live for ever.

70. FOR OUR LORD'S INTERCESSION.

O Lover of the souls of men, in thy
great mercy remember me, thy unworthy
servant, where now thou makest inter-
cession for us at the right hand of God.

71. FOR THE SICK AND SUFFERING.

Receive into the arms of thy mercy, O
Lord, the sick and the suffering, especially

those that I know and love. Heal them,
O Christ, as thou hast promised, from
all evil both of soul and of body, and
raise them up to serve thee with new and
thankful hearts, O thou who art the maker
and redeemer of us all.

72. FOR THE DYING.

At this hour, O Lord, some souls pass
from this life into the unknown world.
May their release be merciful, and may
they find light in thee, who art the God
of all flesh and the Victor over the grave.

73. FOR THE SLEEPLESS.

Close the eyes of the wakeful, most
blessed Lord, with thy gentle touch,
giving them the rest and security that
abide in thy nearness, O thou in whom
there is no night and no darkness.

74. FOR THOSE IN DANGER.

Into the hands of thy mercy, O Lord, I
commit all those who are in danger; uphold and protect them in thy love, I pray
thee, giving them that courage and en-
durance that come from a knowledge of
thy care; through Jesus Christ our Lord.

75. FOR THE AGED.

O God, give thy undimming light to
all those who come towards the evening of
their earthly life, brightening their days

with the serenity of a whole-hearted faith in thy love.

76. For One Preparing to Undergo an Operation.

Bless thy servant, O Lord God, and grant to *him* the strength that is needful. Give the surgeons and nurses thy grace, that by their ministrations thy will may be accomplished in loving service.

77. For Those in Doubt and Darkness.

O God, shatter the prison bars of doubt and set free all thy people who sit in darkness. Shine with thy true light upon them and bring them forth with joy to the freedom of thy presence; through Christ our Lord.

78. For All who are Worried and Afraid.

O blessed Jesus, smooth away the cares from those who are anxious, and lead them into the paths of thy peace, where all their fears shall be lost in the brightness of thy love.

79. For All Those who have Given up Praying.

Forgive and bless, O Lord, those who have given up coming to thee in prayer. In thy mercy look upon them and draw

them to thee, that they may feel their
need and seek thee once again.

80. FOR THOSE WHO HAVE NONE TO PRAY FOR THEM.

Accept my prayers, dear Father, for
those who have no one to love them
enough to pray for them. Wherever and
whoever they are, give them a share of
my blessings, and in thy love let them
know that they are not forgotten.

81. FOR THE HOMELESS AND THE HUNGRY.

Lord Jesus, I pray thee to succour all
those who have nowhere to go; no bed, no
comfort, and no food. Stir us all to do
for them what we profess to be willing to
do for thee, and give them speedy relief.

82. FOR THOSE WHO HAVE BAD HOMES.

O thou who didst honour the homes of
thy friends with thy gracious presence,
bless, I pray thee, all thy children who live
in surroundings of evil and horror. Put
it into the hearts of thy servants to labour
devotedly for the improvement of home
life, that we may all have a place where
happiness and love may rule in thy Name.

83. FOR THOSE WHO ARE LOSING HOPE.

Defend with thy strength, O God, all
thy children who, overcome by the diffi-

culties and perplexities of life, are losing hope. Give them a new vision of thy love that they may see again what they fear to have lost, and grant that what they see they may long for, trusting in thee for its fulfilment.

84. For Those who Lack Courage to Make a Fresh Start.

O thou who art the giver of all good things, grant to those who are discouraged the grace to start anew. Give them the assurance of thy help, that they may put the past behind them and press forward to the goal of thy promises; through the love of Jesus Christ.

85. For Those who Feel Forgotten by God.

Shine in the hearts and minds of those who think themselves forgotten by thee, O God. Hear our prayers for all who are in spiritual darkness and the shadow of what is worse than death, and in thy mercy guide their steps into the way of thy peace.

86. For Those who have no Work.

O God, I pray for all who have no regular work. Give them grace to hope again, and put into the hearts of employers the will and the ability to provide honest and decent work, that the bitterness of idleness may be taken away for ever.

87. FOR THE WEALTHY AND THE PENNILESS.

Dear Lord, I pray thee to help those who have too much, that they may free themselves of some of their burden; and those who have too little, that their wants may be filled; granting that we may see in our time a better way of life, where such unfairness of opportunity can no longer exist.

88. FOR SQUARE PEGS IN ROUND HOLES.

Eternal Father, give thy blessing to all those who are in unsuitable positions; giving thy strength to those who must endure for a while, and thy blessing to those who need the courage to change their way of life; that they all may serve thee according to thy will and purpose.

89. FOR THOSE WHO ARE WORRIED ABOUT MONEY.

Heavenly Father, give thy comfort to all those who are in need and who are concerned for providing the means of life, that they may have such a trust in the care of thy providence that they may serve thee with an untroubled mind.

90. For the Selfish.

Help us, Lord Jesus, to see how narrow our world is when we are concerned with our own affairs, and give us something of thy great love for others, that in loving them we may forget ourselves.

91. For all who have the Care of Animals.

To those who have animals in their care, O Lord, give patience and gentleness; and help us all to remember that thou hast created these, our little brethren, and to treat them accordingly.

92. For Friends and Loved Ones.

Bless, O my God, all who are dear to me, that, loving one another in thee, we may find how near we are in thy love.

93. For all who Keep us Safe.

Defend, O Lord, all who defend us, and guard those who guard our safety; that being kept from all violence we may gratefully serve thee in peace and security.

94. For Travellers.

Keep in safety, O Lord, I pray thee, all who travel. Bring them in peace to the end of their earthly journeys, and at the last bring us all in joy to the haven where we would be.

95. For Teachers.

Bless, O Lord, all who teach; grant to them a patient and loving understanding, and give them the joy of seeing the fruits of their labours in sincere and happy lives.

96. For Courageous Thinkers.

Almighty God, send us, I pray thee, brave and clear thinkers to lead us; give them courage and boldness to fight for the best and highest, and help us all to give them our sincere and thoughtful support.

97. For Those who Learn.

God bless all children at school, and all others who learn; giving them honest teachers and a real desire to seek the truth, using their learning to the bettering of the world in thy service.

98. For Those who Guide the Opinions of Others.

Grant, O Lord, to all who guide the public opinion, all writers, speakers and teachers, that they may seek first the truth and forget their own advantage, that thy people may be kept from all party strife and all narrowness of outlook; through Christ our Lord.

99. For the Queen and the Government.

O God, bless thy servant our Queen, and grant to her and to all her ministers the counsel of thy Spirit, that this great people may be ruled in justice and righteousness and may be enabled to live in peace, to thy honour and glory.

100. For Newcomers to the Parish.

Bless with thy peaceful presence those who have come to be my neighbours, O Lord; and give me grace to be of service to them for thy sake.

101. For Peace.

O Eternal Father, give peace to the aching hearts of men. Stir us all, O God, to seek thee and thy peace in everything that we think and do, and so stablish thy rule and thy kingdom amongst us; through Jesus Christ our Lord.

102. For a House or Room.

Almighty and merciful God, bless with thy presence this place, casting out all evil, and leaving thy abiding presence herein.